STICKMEN'S GUIDE TO CITIES
– UNCOVERED

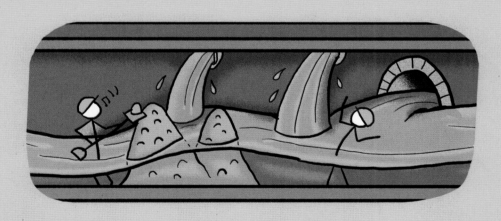

by Catherine Chambers
Illustrated by John Paul de Quay

HUNGRY
TOMATO™

Contents

Cities

The most successful cities in the world attract millions of people. New arrivals and new businesses put pressure on land. This is why our biggest cities are built ever upwards – and down below ground level. This book takes a look at what happens from the very top to the underground depths, and the layers in between.

Reaching for the Sky

City skyscrapers soar higher and higher but no space is wasted, even at the top! The wind, sun and great views are used to the full.

High Power

From the top, elevators and escalators whisk you down from floor to floor, powered by electric cables hidden behind walls and ceilings.

Along the Ground

You can walk, cycle or take the bus or tram along bustling city streets. Shiny shop windows and dazzling neon lights make the big city sparkle.

Underground

For speedy travel, take the underground train. Also down under lie hidden networks of cabling and entire water and sewage systems.

On Top of the World

Architects test their skyscraper designs in wind tunnels to make sure the tops can cope with high winds. They build in curves and fins to reduce the impact. But they also make use of those dizzy heights and stiff breezes!

Satellite dishes

Communication mast

Getting the message

Communications are key to running a city. Clear signals are vital, so the tops of skyscrapers are ideal for siting telecommunications equipment. These include antennae that receive radio waves, and transmitters that emit them. Sky-high satellite dishes receive signals from satellites orbiting Earth in the upper atmosphere.

Solar panels

Soaking up the sun

The top of a tall building is the perfect place to capture the sun's energy. There are fewer tightly packed buildings to create shadows. Here, panels of photovoltaic cells (solar panels) can be positioned to get maximum exposure to the sun all day. This is a sustainable way to make electricity.

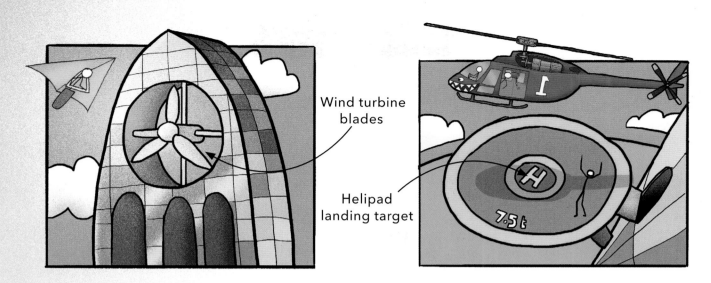

Wind turbine blades

Helipad landing target

7.5 t

Catching the wind

This wind turbine at the top of a tower in Dubai is integrated into the building. Its clever design makes the turbine more stable in winds that can reach 150 km/h (90 mph). Skyscrapers in many cities worldwide have to include a sustainable source of energy in their design, as here.

High helipad

Flying in helicopters is a neat way of avoiding city traffic. More importantly, firefighters can land close to flames engulfing the tops of skyscrapers. The highest helipad sits on top of China's Guangzhou International Finance Center. Here, helicopters land 438 m (1,439 feet) above the streets below.

Fun at the Top

Skyscrapers are expensive to build. Dubai's Burj Khalifa, the tallest building in the world, cost £990 million ($1.5 billion). So investors and architects make sure that their rooftops are not wasted. They take full advantage of the view, if you dare look!

Parks in the sky

There's a lot of luxury on top of modern skyrise buildings. In Singapore, Marina Bay Sands Sky Park is a 340-m-long (1,115-ft) entertainment space. It has 250 shade trees, a 150-m (492-ft) infinity swimming pool and restaurants overlooking the South China Sea.

Sky sports

Miniature golf courses, tennis courts and running tracks can all be laid out on top of tall buildings, as this pitch and putt course has been. Sky-high sports lovers might be surprised by an urban free-climber appearing suddenly over the railings! These climbers use no safety gear to scale city skyscrapers.

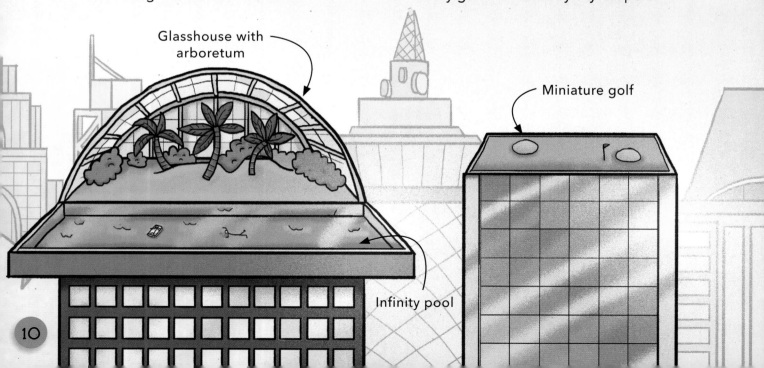

Glasshouse with arboretum

Miniature golf

Infinity pool

Flying fairground

Hair-raising chair rides like this are suspended from skyscraper rooftops and rotate around them. Polercoaster, a new high-rise roller-coaster design, has a 1,584-m (5,200-ft) track that whizzes riders around at 100 km/h (65 mph). It is due to open in 2017 on a retail complex in Orlando, Florida, USA.

Greening the city
Plants grown in rooftop gardens help to absorb cities' polluting gases. They release more oxygen into the air for people to breathe, too.

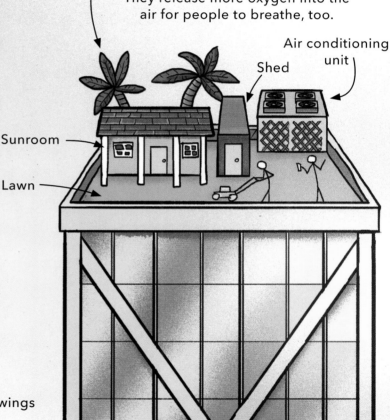

Air conditioning unit

Shed

Sunroom

Lawn

Sheds on top

High-rise roofs are not always topped by sleek restaurants and pools. Among air-conditioning vents and water tanks, some city-dwellers build ramshackle sheds, sunrooms, greenhouses, vegetable beds and even beehives. Some rooftops are planted with succulent species that need no artificial watering.

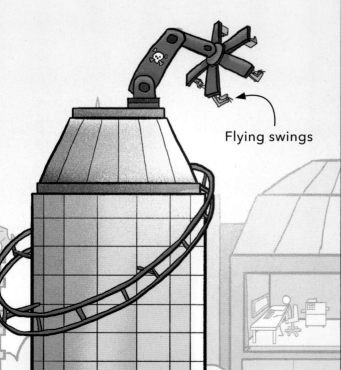

Flying swings

Going Down...

Skyscrapers would be unusable without lifts, or elevators, to take you down from the top – or up from below. The lifts in China's new CTF Finance Center in Guangzhou city can descend at 20 m (65 ft) per second!

Elevators on the edge

Elevators take up precious space inside narrow city buildings. So some are built on the outside, like this one on the Lloyds Building in London, UK.

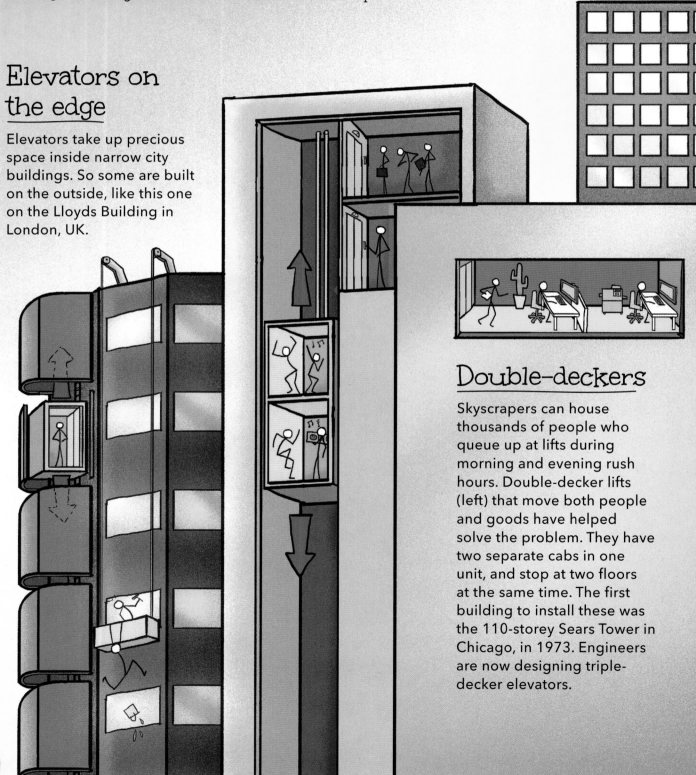

Double-deckers

Skyscrapers can house thousands of people who queue up at lifts during morning and evening rush hours. Double-decker lifts (left) that move both people and goods have helped solve the problem. They have two separate cabs in one unit, and stop at two floors at the same time. The first building to install these was the 110-storey Sears Tower in Chicago, in 1973. Engineers are now designing triple-decker elevators.

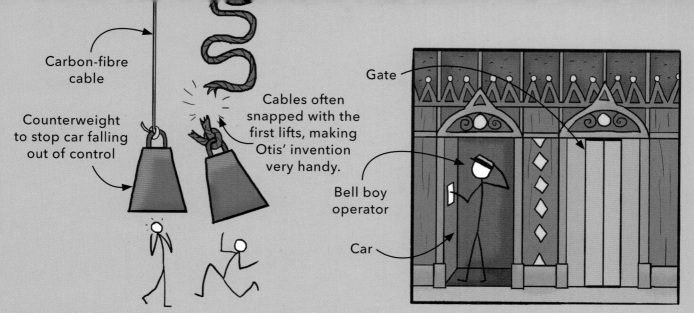

Carbon-fibre cable

Counterweight to stop car falling out of control

Cables often snapped with the first lifts, making Otis' invention very handy.

Gate

Bell boy operator

Car

Super-cables

Tough steel cables raise and lower most lifts today. But superstrong, lightweight carbon-fibre cables, and belts coated with tough polyurethane, are being developed to replace them. Engineers are designing new braking systems to serve skyscrapers 1,000 m (3,300 ft) tall. Lifts can fall at 20 m/sec (72 km/h or 45 mph)!

The first elevator

Elevator design dates back to 236BCE in Ancient Greece. But American Elisha Graves Otis introduced the first safety lift in 1854. This was a spring-loaded device that caught the lift platform should it fall. In the 20th century, piston-powered hydraulic lifts were designed for low-rise buildings.

Testing, testing

Engineers use computer simulation to design the lofty lifts of the future. But in Finland, the Kone company has plunged a 305-m (1,000-ft) test lift shaft down into a limestone mine. Here, experimental elevators are tested at speeds of up to 17 m/sec (56 ft/sec).

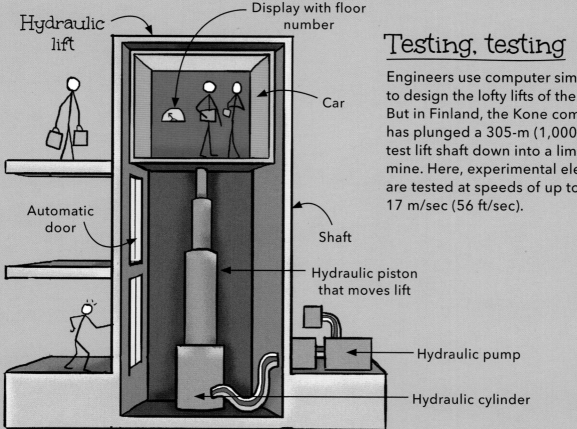

Hydraulic lift

Display with floor number

Car

Automatic door

Shaft

Hydraulic piston that moves lift

Hydraulic pump

Hydraulic cylinder

High Power

Bright city lights that reach to the rooftops need constant power. So do vital safety systems, such as fire alarms, sprinklers, CCTV cameras and burglar alarms. Offices need power and fibre-optic cables for computer and Internet links.

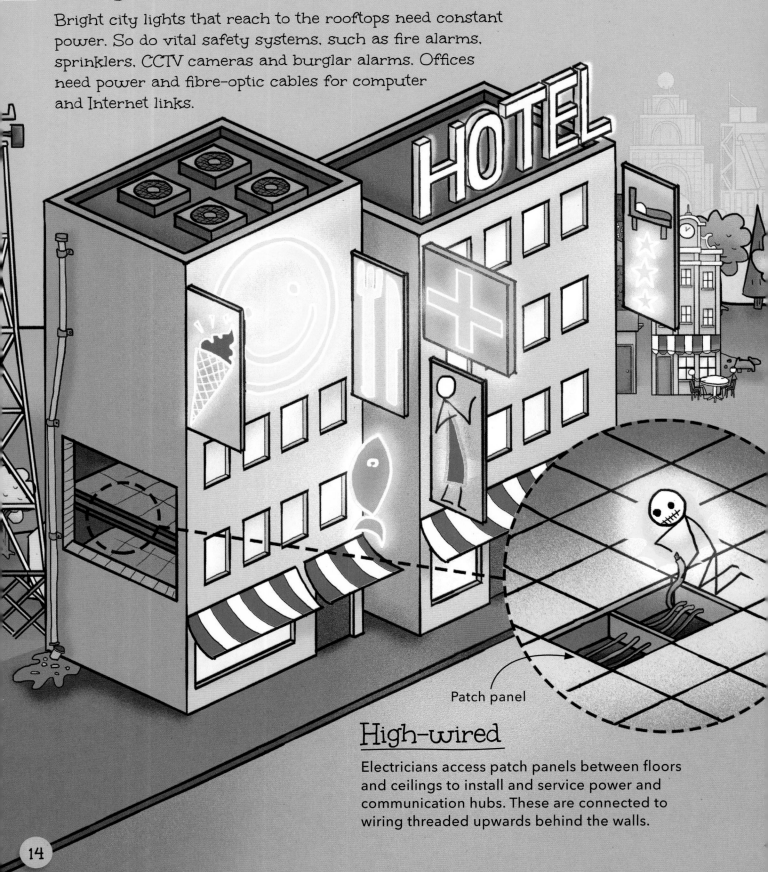

Patch panel

High-wired

Electricians access patch panels between floors and ceilings to install and service power and communication hubs. These are connected to wiring threaded upwards behind the walls.

The largest screen

Brightly lit screens advertising stores and shows dazzle high above city streets everywhere. New York City's Times Square boasts a screen that spans a whole block. It stretches from 45th to 46th Street, reaches eight storeys high, and gleams with nearly 24 million LED (Light Emitting Diode) pixels.

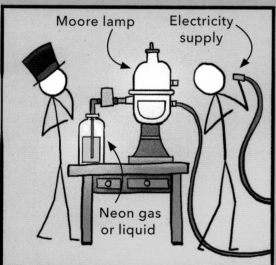

Moore lamp

Electricity supply

Neon gas or liquid

Bright lights

Tall buildings and narrow streets made cities very dark at night until about 100 years ago. They lit up after Frenchman Georges Claude discovered that passing electricity through neon gas or liquid produced a bright red light. He confined the light inside a Moore lamp, and the neon light was born.

LED bulbs

LED revolution

LEDs are bright spots of light produced by electricity, known as electroluminescence. They are often no bigger than a pinhead. Millions of these tiny red, green and blue LED pixels together can create glowing multi-coloured images and words. They can move, too! LED bulbs are more energy-efficient than neon or fluorescent lights and are used to illuminate streets.

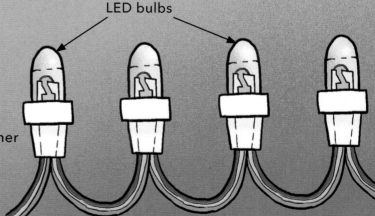

A Slice of Life

High-rise floors in the city can open up into vast workspaces. In department stores, internal escalators expose the whole space vertically. As customers travel up and down, they can take a snapshot view of each floor's displays and in-store advertising.

Endless choice

In the 1880s, the first open-plan, multi-storey department stores amazed their customers. Today, the biggest store is Shinsegae in Busan, South Korea, at more than 288,000 m² (3,100,000 sq ft).

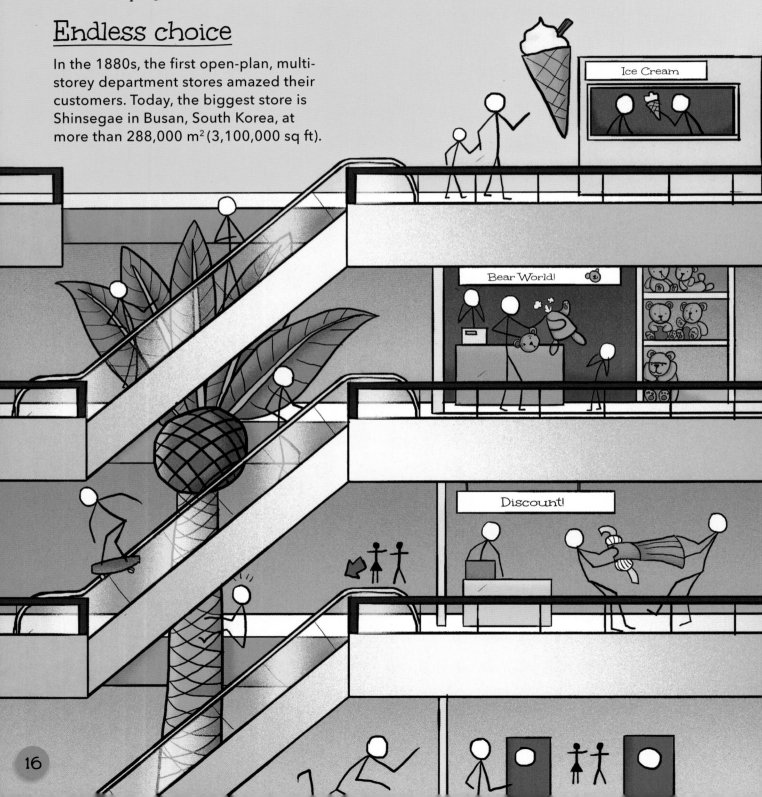

Ice Cream

Bear World!

Discount!

Easy networking

Open-plan offices (left) allow easily linked work hubs, reducing the cost of installing and maintaining communications networks. Workers can communicate with each other quickly, and can be supervised closely. Many employees are now encouraged to personalize their work hubs so they do not all look the same.

Computer-linked work hub

Early open plan

In the early 1900s, the number of office workers expanded, especially in mail-order firms, banks and insurance companies. Efficient, bright, 'work-pool' office design was needed. So the American mechanical engineer, Frederick Winslow Taylor (1856–1915), created the 'Taylorist Open Plan' concept. Workers were crammed together in a large space, performing small, repetitive tasks.

The 1904 design of the Larkin Soap Company's office in the USA by Frank Lloyd Wright used the Taylorist Open Plan idea.

Floor plan

Office desk position

Noisy neighbours

Sound travels vertically between floors but cavity flooring solutions reduce the problem. Square floor panels that rest on short columns allow a gap, or cavity, between the floor and the ceiling below. The gap absorbs loud sounds, and carpeting on top of it adds extra insulation.

Carpet to dull sound

Cavity sound insulation

On the Streets

Glamorous shop windows, cosy cafés and bustling pavements
make the city's ground level a very attractive place. But
pedestrians have to deal with cars, buses, trams and bicycles
streaming by. Noise and fumes fill the air in many large cities.

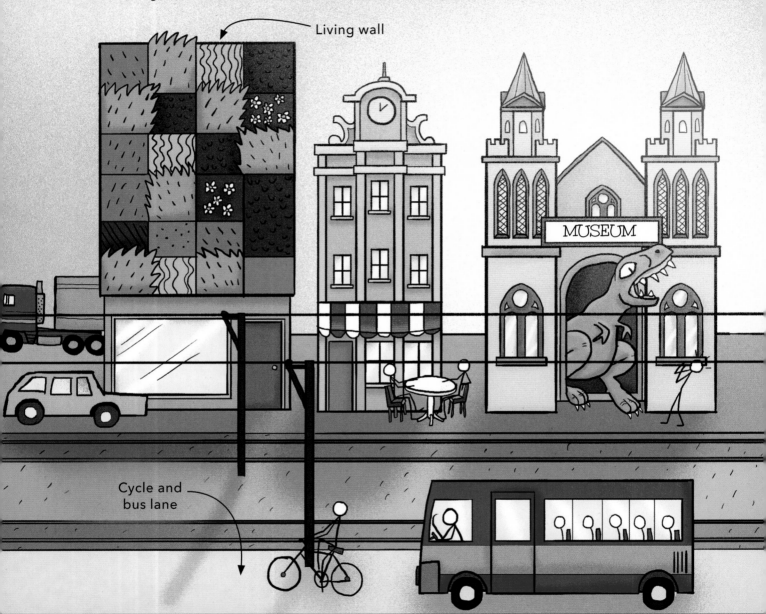

Living wall

Cycle and
bus lane

MUSEUM

Living walls

City pollution is a huge health problem. Walls of plants that absorb carbon gases from
vehicles help clean the air and look great, too. France's Patrick Blanc, an artist and
botanist, began this trend 30 years ago. The plants are rooted to soil held in a mesh
and are watered automatically.

Rattling trams

Trams are carriages on tracks, powered by electrified overhead wires. First used in Russia in the 1880s, they are quieter and cleaner than motorized vehicles. They will be even cleaner when all trams use new wire-free supercapacitors. These are stores of electricity released to power the tram.

Quiet tracks

Tram tracks clatter. So in some cities, grass is laid between the tracks to dampen the sound. The grass also absorbs carbon pollution in the air. In Rotterdam in the Netherlands, street surfaces are now made of 'quiet asphalt' to reduce vehicle noise.

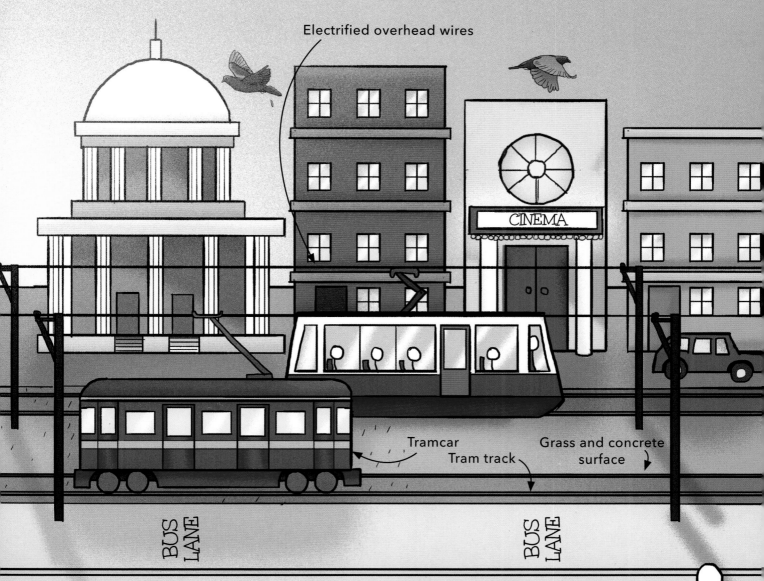

Electrified overhead wires

CINEMA

Tramcar
Tram track

Grass and concrete surface

BUS LANE

BUS LANE

Flood danger

Heavy rain runs off the city's hard concrete and tarmac surfaces, filling drains and flooding streets. Grasscrete (openwork concrete paving with grass centres) allows water to soak away.

Openwork concrete shapes with porous grass pockets

Power under our Feet

Below the city streets, networks of cables bring light, heat and communications to billions of people. Above ground, these wires would be exposed to snow, ice and high winds. The first underground cabling was laid 150 years ago.

The price of power

Installing power below our streets can be dangerous work and disrupts busy pedestrians. It is also expensive. Underground electric cables cost between five and ten times more to install than those above ground. Repairing them can cost 60 per cent more.

Bending light

Office computers and cash registers operate by using signal transmitters called optical fibres. These thin tubes of high-quality glass carry information as light rays that seem to 'bend' as they move, by bouncing along the tubes.

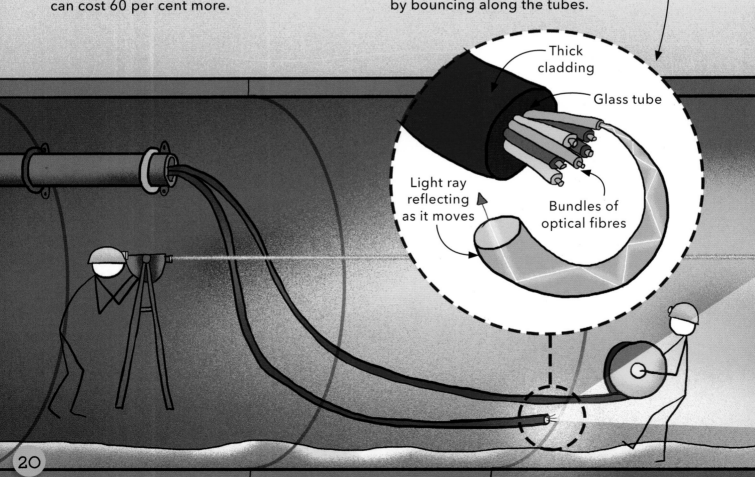

Thick cladding

Glass tube

Light ray reflecting as it moves

Bundles of optical fibres

Laying cables

Cables are pushed into position using rods, or pulled by winches. The jetting technique pushes cables through with a rush of air. This helps to stop them from sticking against pipes or other cables. 'Floating' the cables in a stream of water prevents buckling and bending as they are fed through.

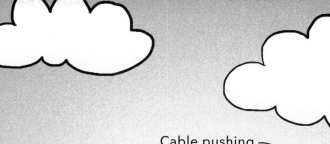

Cable pushing machine

Live electricity wire

Gnaw, really?

When power is cut, engineers often find that the cable jackets have been gnawed through. This is the work of mice, rats and gophers trying to sharpen their teeth! Solutions include a steel coating on the cables, or treating them with capsaicin, a burning chemical found in chilli peppers!

Cable casing or ducting

Digging deep

Our growing cities need more and more cable networks. It means digging further down or expanding the tunnels that carry them. Engineers must then ensure that cables can take the increased pressure from above. They do this with heavy insulation, pipes and ducting around the cables.

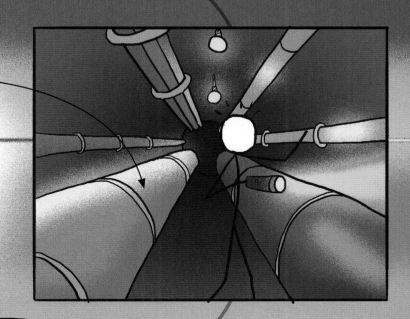

Keeping Clean

Deep underground, millions of gallons of water are pumped up into the city, where it is used in all kinds of ways, then drained away again. Underground sewage systems were first developed in the ancient cities of the Indus Valley (now in Pakistan) in 2500BCE.

Rising water

In a flood, water gushes through sewers and up into the streets. Many cities are built on the coast or on river floodplains, and are expanding. This puts pressure on both the water table (the underground water level) and pumps that carry away excess water. Excessive rainfall during torrential storms will push a city's sewage system to its limits.

Facing fatbergs

Fatbergs are huge balls of fat that slow the flow of our sewage systems. They solidify from cooking fats washed down millions of sinks. In 2013, a sewage worker in Kingston, UK, found a fatberg as big as two African elephants! It was 95 per cent the height of the sewer pipe itself.

Fatberg containing waste

Stop that leak!

Leaking pipes, or water line breaks, in the water system are a costly waste. In the USA, $2.8 billion (£1.85 billion) a year is spent fixing them. Water engineers access pipes through cast iron manhole covers set into pavements. They close shut-off valves between lengths of supply pipes to find which one is broken.

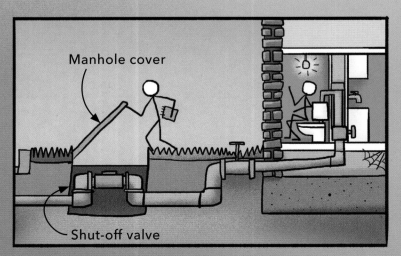

Manhole cover

Shut-off valve

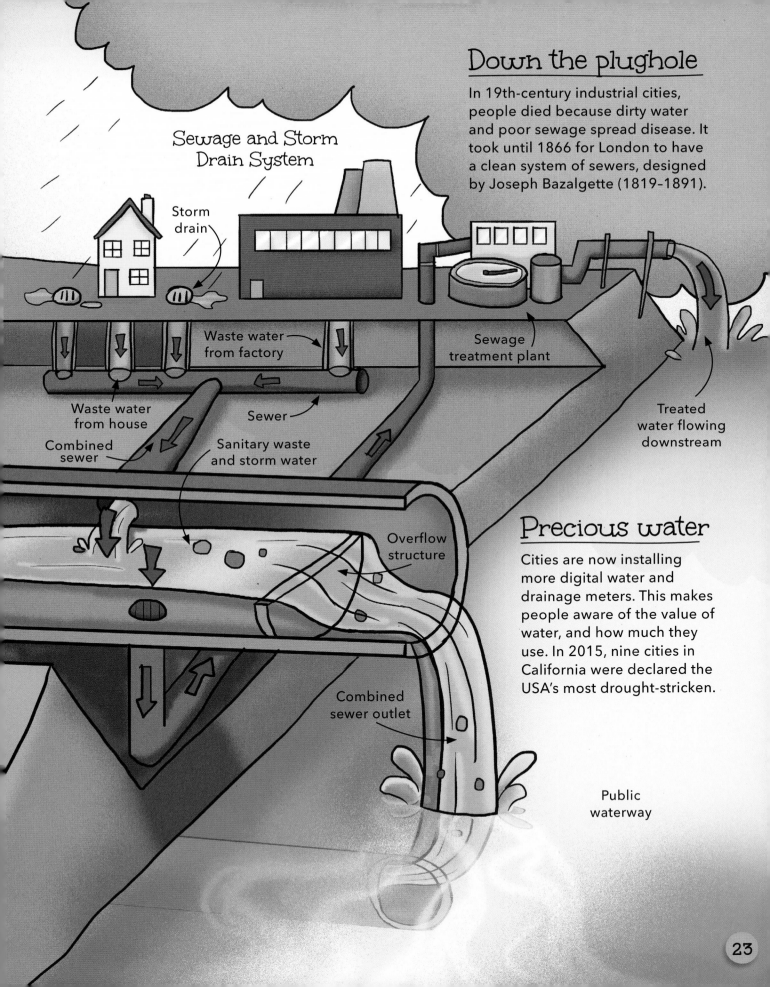

Down the plughole

In 19th-century industrial cities, people died because dirty water and poor sewage spread disease. It took until 1866 for London to have a clean system of sewers, designed by Joseph Bazalgette (1819–1891).

Sewage and Storm Drain System

Storm drain

Waste water from factory

Sewage treatment plant

Treated water flowing downstream

Waste water from house

Sewer

Combined sewer

Sanitary waste and storm water

Overflow structure

Precious water

Cities are now installing more digital water and drainage meters. This makes people aware of the value of water, and how much they use. In 2015, nine cities in California were declared the USA's most drought-stricken.

Combined sewer outlet

Public waterway

Travel Below Ground

Underground metros, or subways, help ease traffic jams and packed pavements in the streets above. One of the most modern is Copenhagen's subway, in Denmark, which runs for 24 hours with driverless trains.

Underground station entrance

Double-decker trains

At peak travel times, metro systems are now as packed as the streets above. Double-decker trains have been introduced to solve overcrowding problems in cities such as Berlin in Germany and Sydney in Australia.

Escalator

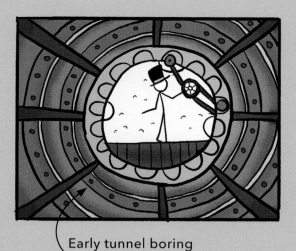

Early tunnel boring machine (TBM)

Tunnelling the tube

The invention of hefty tunnel boring machines (TBMs) made it possible to carve out the first underground. Today's TBMs are surprisingly similar in design, but much longer, like a factory in a tube. In London, the new Crossrail underground needed eight TBMs, each about as long as two Airbus 380 airliners. They dug down 40 m (131 ft) beneath the streets.

First metro

In 1890, the City and South London Railway opened the world's first deep-level, electrified underground railway, or metro. A masterpiece of engineering, it ran from north to south London through a tunnel built under the River Thames. The locomotives were small to fit the narrow tunnels, and could haul three coaches at speeds of up to 40 km/h (25 mph).

Subway facts box

Most stations	New York, USA (422)
Most lines	New York, USA (24)
Longest track	Shanghai, China 538 km (334 miles)
Most passengers	Beijing, China (over 10 million a day)
Deepest station	Arsenalna station in Kiev, Ukraine (107 m/351 ft)

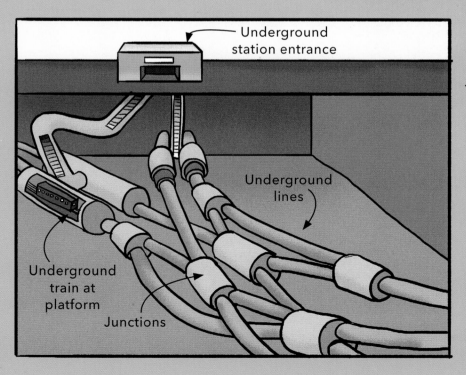

Underground station entrance

Underground lines

Underground train at platform

Junctions

Planning the lines

Subway lines converging on a single station require careful planning. Junctions join lines as they approach a platform. Here, signals stop trains on different lines from accessing a platform at the same time. New lines weave through existing ones, avoiding sewers, power supplies and underground rivers.

Down Under

Foundations reach down to the deepest layer of our cities. They support the increasing number and height of multi-storey buildings. New foundation technologies allow construction on what was once seen as unstable, unsuitable land.

Caisson pile

Steel rod reinforcement

Floating foundation

Bedrock   Soil

Pile walls made of steel

Sinking feeling

Soft soils make normal foundations sink. But large, flat floating foundations that support high-rise buildings allow them just to shift slightly as the earth gives way. Clay is a soft soil, but only when wet. When dry, it shrinks, causing buildings above to subside. So deep supporting piles are driven below the clay.

Pushing down piles

Tall buildings are held up by long supports called piles, which are driven by machinery into the bedrock. Caissons are massive cylindrical piles reinforced by steel rods. They are at least 1 m (3 ft 3 in) in diameter. Steel sheet pile walls help keep soil and rubble around them from shifting.

Deepest foundations

Malaysia's Petronas Twin Towers soar 452 m (1,483 ft) above street level. They are so tall that their pinnacles house aircraft warning lights. They sit on foundations of reinforced concrete held up by 104 supporting rods, or piles. Some of these reach down 114 m (374 ft) and are the deepest in the world.

Hitting water

The water table is the natural level of water beneath us. In many cities, foundations that are in contact with the water table push the level up, so it might lie only a few feet below. On construction sites, pumps remove excess water constantly. The basements of buildings can then be built from concrete encased by steel as a barrier to water.

Rocking with the shock

Buildings set on rigid foundations crack in an earthquake. So new skyscrapers are designed to rock with the shock waves. They rest on foundations fitted with isolators, or flexible pads, that lift or 'isolate' them above the ground and allow them to lean. At the top of the building, a heavy weight swings in a harness to rebalance the structure if it lurches too much to one side.

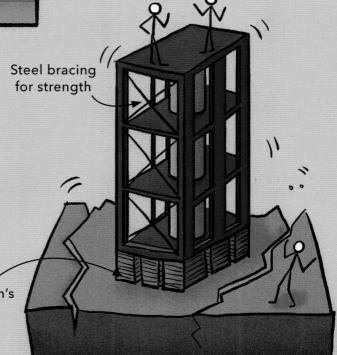

Steel bracing for strength

Foundation's isolator

Fantastic City Facts

High-rise Hong Kong

Hong Kong, in south-east China, has an amazing 1,268 skyscrapers, with more being built all the time. New York has 684, the second largest number. Hong Kong is a bustling commercial city built on a small island and islets in the Pearl River delta. It spreads outwards on reclaimed land, but building upwards is still vital to the city's prosperity.

Top tennis

In 2005, tennis stars Andrei Agassi of the USA and Switzerland's Roger Federer played a match on a helipad – at the top of Dubai's Burj Al Arab hotel, 210 m (689 ft) in the air. The tennis court lies within the helipad's circle, which perches below the very top of this 321-m (1,053-ft) tall hotel.

One large plan

In 2015, Facebook moved into the largest open-plan office in the world, in Menlo Park, California. It was designed to house 3,400 engineers, all working in the same space, though there are smaller, quiet areas, too. The roof dips and rises like a wave, 14–22 m (45–73 ft) above ground, with trees planted on the top.

Triple lifts

Engineers have designed a triple-decker elevator to take people up and down the new wave of super-skyscrapers. They are so tall that they have to stop at two floors at a time. Designers need to reduce the weight of these lifts, with their ropes and pulleys, to allow them to move – and fast!

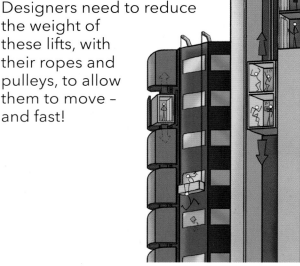

City cycling

Down at street level, cyclists compete with trams and traffic. But things are not so bad for cyclists in Copenhagen, Denmark. Here, there are over 390 km (242 miles) of cycle track. Copenhagen is regularly voted the 'Best Bike City in the World'. In winter, cycle tracks are cleared of snow before roads. Bikes rule!

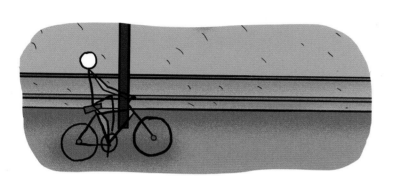

Time at the top

If you need to know the time in Makkah (Mecca), Saudi Arabia, just look up at the Royal Clock Tower Hotel, in the Abraj Al Bait complex. Its four-sided clock is 601 m (1,972 ft) high and can be seen 25 km (15 miles) away.

Tallest 'living wall'

The living wall growing inside the Desjardins office building in Levis, Quebec, rises 65 m (213 ft) inside a glass atrium. It has 11,000 plants with 42 different species, including ginger, fig trees and banana plants. They are not rooted in soil but fed with water containing nutrients.

Snake in the sewers

In 2015, in Manchester, UK, a snake kept popping up in bathrooms from deep in the sewers. Fibre-optic equipment was fed underground but the snake was nowhere to be seen. Finally, the 3-m (10-ft) boa constrictor was spotted again in a bathroom and caught in a bucket. Its name was Keith.

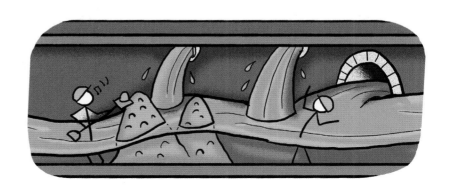

The Future...

More and more people are living in cities and the only way they can expand is up – and down. In the future they might look like layers of streets in the sky. Buildings might reach so high that the air is too thin to breathe outside them.

New designs

Most tall city buildings taper at the top. This affects the way they are used, with department stores or car parking spaces at the bottom, and offices and apartments at the thinner peaks. New mushroom-shaped designs are allowing greater, more versatile space in the upper layers.

Night sky

Light pollution prevents city dwellers from enjoying a dark, starlit sky that is highly visible in the countryside. Street lamps with new LED bulbs use less energy and glow with a softer light, which is filtered to reduce glare. Hooded shades point light beams down, improving the quality of the darkness in the city.

Windy cities

Increased wind speeds and flooding may threaten safety in our cities. Engineers and architects are designing materials and structures that can withstand them. Tall buildings add to the problem of wind by creating a downdraught. In a cyclone, wind travelling between high-rise structures creates a fast-spinning vortex.

New ways of living

Maybe in future there will be so many city dwellers that they will occupy high-rise layers connected by walkways and cycleways. Or they will live underground. Architects are designing skyscrapers made of shipping containers as temporary housing. And in cities near the sea, such as Lagos in Nigeria, new artificial islands are being created for people to live and work on.

Glossary

Asphalt

Building material made of stones and fillers bound with bitumen tar

Carbon fibre

Strengthening material made of fine carbon threads

Cavity

Gap or space

Grasscrete

Concrete mosaic with patches of grass that allow drainage

Insulation

Material or space that keeps in sound or heat

Isolator

Support that allows the building above to move

Junction

Where two lines meet

Loading gauge

Height limit for tunnels taking subway trains

Manhole cover

Strong cast iron door to underground storm drains and sewers

Neon

Gas or liquid that makes a coloured light when electricity is passed through it

Orbiting

Circling an object

Patch panel

Square unit that can be opened up to install or fix equipment behind it

Photovoltaic cell

Cell that can convert energy from the sun into electricity

Pile

Long, strong rod that holds up a building

Polyurethane

Strong plastic material

Spring-loaded

Spring that presses one part of an object against the other

Supercapacitor

Quick-charging electricity store that uses static electricity

Succulent

Fleshy-leaved plant that needs little watering

INDEX

The Author

Catherine Chambers was born in Adelaide, South Australia, grew up in the UK, and studied African History and Swahili at the School of Oriental and African Studies in London. She has written about 130 books for children and young adults, and enjoys seeking out intriguing facts for her non-fiction titles, which cover history, cultures, faiths, biography, geography and the environment.

The Illustrator

John Paul de Quay has a BSc in Biology from the University of Sussex, UK, and a graduate certificate in animation from the University of the West of England. He devotes his spare time to growing chilli peppers, perfecting his plan for a sustainable future and caring for a small plastic dinosaur. He has three pet squid that live in the bath, which makes drawing in ink quite economical …